CW00952691

I READ!
YOU READ!

Child's Turn to Read

Adult's Turn to Read

WE READ ABOUT

BABY ELEPHANTS

Amy Culliford and Madison Parker

TABLE OF CONTENTS

SEAHORSE
PUBLISHING

Parent and Caregiver Guide

Reading aloud with your child has many benefits. It expands vocabulary, sparks discussion, and promotes an emotional bond. Research shows that children who have books read aloud to them have improved language skills, leading to greater school success.

I Read! You Read! books offer a fun and easy way to read with your child. Follow these guidelines.

Before Reading

- Look at the front and back covers. Discuss personal experiences that relate to the topic.
- Read the *Words to Know* on page 3. Talk about what the words mean.
- If the book will be challenging or unfamiliar to your child, read it aloud by yourself the first time. Then, invite your child to participate in a second reading.

During Reading

CHILD

Have your child read the words beside this symbol. This text has been carefully matched to the reading and grade levels shown on the cover.

ADULT

You read the words beside this symbol.

- Stop often to discuss what you are reading and to make sure your child understands.
- If your child struggles with decoding a word, help them sound it out. If it is still a challenge, say the word for your child and have them repeat it after you.
- To find the meaning of a word, look for clues in the surrounding words and pictures.

After Reading

- Praise your child's efforts. Notice how they have grown as a reader.
- Ask and answer questions about the book.
- Discuss what your child learned and what they liked or didn't like about the book.

Most importantly, let your child know that reading is fun and worthwhile. Keep reading together as your child's skills and confidence grow.

WORDS TO KNOW

 baby elephant

 ears

 gray

 milk

 trunk

SIGHT WORDS

a	from	like	play	to
all	get	long	some	
are	have	most	their	
big	is	mother	this	

3

This is a **baby elephant.**

CHILD

Baby elephants are mammals. Mammals have fur and make milk for their babies.

ADULT

4

baby elephant

Some baby elephants are **gray**.

CHILD

There are three species of elephants: African Savanna, African Forest, and Asian. All can be **gray**.

ADULT

gray

Baby elephants get **milk** from their mother.

CHILD

Baby elephants drink **milk** for the first six months of life.

ADULT

milk

Most baby elephants **CHILD** have big **ears**.

Elephants have big **ears** that release body heat. **ADULT**

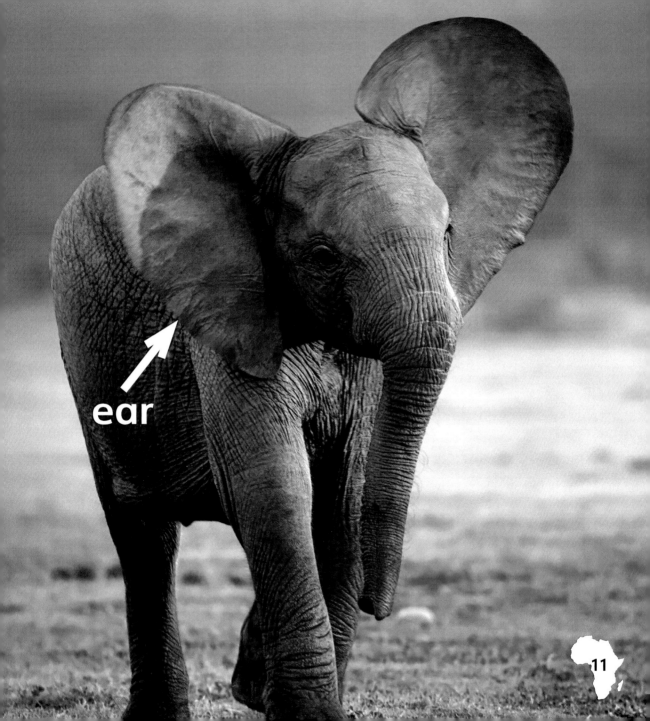

ear

All baby elephants CHILD
have a long **trunk**.

A baby elephant's **trunk** helps it drink water and take a bath. ADULT

trunk →

13

All baby elephants like to play!

CHILD

Some baby elephants like to chase and wrestle each other.

ADULT

14

Index

Written by: Amy Culliford and Madison Parker
Design by: Under the Oaks Media
Series Development: James Earley
Editor: Kim Thompson

Photos: Johann Marais: cover; Charmaine Jabert: p. 4-5; Steve Lagreca: p. 7; Graeme Shannon: p. 8-9; Johan Swanepoel: p. 11; Edwin Butter: p. 13; Africa Wildlife: p. 15

Library of Congress PCN Data
We Read About Baby Elephants / Amy Culliford and Madison Parker
I Read! You Read!
ISBN 979-8-8873-5182-7 (hard cover)
ISBN 979-8-8873-5202-2 (paperback)
ISBN 979-8-8873-5222-0 (EPUB)
ISBN 979-8-8873-5242-8 (eBook)
Library of Congress Control Number: 2022945542

Printed in the United States of America.

Seahorse Publishing Company

www.seahorsepub.com   1-800-387-7650

Published in the United States
Seahorse Publishing
PO Box 771325
Coral Springs, FL 33077

SEAHORSE PUBLISHING